FOREST
FORENSICS

T0021794

FOREST FORENSICS

A FIELD GUIDE TO READING THE FORESTED LANDSCAPE

TOM WESSELS

Countryman Press

An Imprint of W. W. Norton & Company
Independent Publishers Since 1923

CIP data are available.

Forest Forensics

ISBN 978-0-88150-918-2

Copyright © 2010 by Tom Wessels

For information about special discounts for bulk purchases, please contact W. W. Norton Special Sales at specialsales@wwnorton.com or 800-233-4830

Interior photographs by the author
Book design and composition by S. E. Livingston

Published by Countryman Press,
www.countrymanpress.com

An imprint of W. W. Norton & Company, Inc.,
500 Fifth Avenue, New York, NY 10110
www.wwnorton.com

Printed in the United States by Versa Press, East Peoria, Illinois

10 9

CONTENTS

Preface

Can I walk through a forest and not interpret its history? I've been asked that question a number of times, suggesting that the need to analyze forest histories may be something that I can't control. Yet the answer is yes. I love to read forested landscapes, but there are definitely times when I place my focus in other directions.

My wife, Marcia, and I live on 35 acres in Westminster, Vermont, the bulk of which is a woodlot that I manage to promote biodiversity, our cordwood supply, and some saw timber. I have developed a 1-mile loop trail through this forest that is smooth and free of anything but leaf litter. The loop is where I run, ski, and take my daily walks.

I use these walks to contemplate, work on my writing, and sometimes even to meditate. At such times reading the forested landscape is the farthest thing from my mind. So it came as a great shock many years ago when I realized that it had taken me over a decade to see the imprint of the 1938 hurricane in our forest. When asked to interpret any other woodland, I would pick up evidence of that hurricane, or the lack thereof, within a matter of minutes. Another shock occurred the day I realized that the bulk of our woodlot was once a grain field, when for years I'd assumed that it had only been pasture. It's ironic that the woodland closest to my heart, the woodland I have grown with for over 30 years, was the woodland that took me the longest to decipher.

Yet through all those years I have learned the rich and full story of this forest. Through that process my connections to it have grown deep like the roots of its trees, and expansive like the mycelium of its golden chanterelles. In short I have developed an intimate relationship with this forest.

Just as intimacy is necessary if we are going to forge close bonds with friends and lovers, it is also necessary if we hope to bond with nature and our place. As one learns to see the history of a local landscape, a deep level of intimacy with place can develop. The story of place comes forth as the landscape reveals its experience through our careful attention. But in order to see and hear this story we need to learn a new language—one we can use to read the landscape.

This new language has nouns, verbs, and adjectives just as a written language does, but its words are things such as small stones in a wall, a hollowed-out stump, or a basal scar on a tree trunk. All of these details can be put together like words on a page to tell rich stories about a forest's past.

As I have grown more intimate with my place I have learned that I am not *apart from* the land, but that I am instead *a part of* it. My actions are entwined in my woodlot's history, and this landscape's history before I came on the scene is infused within me. We, the forest and I, are truly connected. It is my hope that users of this guide will find that it will not only help them engage in a fun read of any woodland, but that it will connect them in a far more intimate way to their own forested landscape.

T.W.

Introduction

Reading a forested landscape might be more accurately termed *forest forensics* since it is similar to gleaning a crime scene for evidence to try to piece together exactly what happened in the past. In the case of forests, the evidence I look for are commonly encountered features such as the shapes of trees, where scars occur on trees, decay patterns in stumps or downed logs, the presence of stone walls, and the general lay of the land. All of these commonly encountered features offer wonderful clues to unraveling detailed forest histories if one knows how to interpret them.

It was in this capacity that I was asked in the spring of 2006 to help interpret the agricultural history of a now wooded parcel of land in the Green Mountain National Forest of Vermont. I was a member of a seven-person archaeological team that was trying to puzzle out some very unusual stonework found on the site.

Since the stonework was unique and on federal lands the decision had been made not to disturb the area through a standard dig; so I was brought in to help infer its history solely from visible evidence. I had been told by the archaeologists before getting there that the unusual stonework consisted of dozens of large, flat-topped—for lack of a better word—cairns that seemed to have no logical purpose unless they were in some way related to the site's past agricultural use.

As we walked around the Forest Service gate to a woods road that cut across the slope of a hill, I started to examine the ground on both sides of the road. Whenever I am working to interpret a forest's past agricultural history in New

England I always start by looking at the ground. I am not looking at the vegetative cover or the nature of the forest litter, but rather I am simply scanning the micro-topography of the ground itself. As I looked uphill from the road I could see large pits and mounds, or what I prefer to call pillows and cradles. These features told me that live trees had been toppled there in the past by either windthrow or snow- and ice-loading.

When a live tree falls in a forest its roots rip out of the ground, excavating the pit, or cradle. The roots, now sticking up into the air, hold the earth removed from the cradle. Over time, as the roots decay the excavated earth is dropped, creating the mound, or pillow. Once formed, the live roots of surrounding trees invade the pillow and cradle, stabilizing them. Large pillows and cradles in New England can still be visible almost a millennium after a tree-toppling event. Since the pillows and cradles on this side of the road were quite large and didn't appear to have been worn down by the hooves of livestock, I began to think that this area had always been forested and never opened for any agricultural use.

As we proceeded on the woods road, the ground downslope—the area that held the cairns—quickly changed. Although sloping moderately, the ground on this side was smooth and even—a clear sign that this area had been plowed at some time in the past, removing its pillows and cradles. Since there was no stone or wire fencing along the previously plowed side of the road, I had evidence to confirm that the uphill side was always forest and not pasture, for a fence would have been needed to contain livestock in a pasture.

In New England, land was plowed for two reasons—to create hay fields or to create crop fields. In the case of a hay field, the site would need to be plowed to remove the pillows and cradles that would get in the way of working a scythe, and then the smoothed ground would be seeded. Hay fields were generally plowed just a few times. Crop fields, however, were plowed every year before planting. As I wandered down into the plowed area I started moving across the slope to see if I would come to a stone wall, knowing that a wall would hold the evidence to confirm if the site was originally a hay field or crop field. Once I knew what the site had been used for I could then assess if the cairns were related to that activity.

Most of this region is covered in glacial till—a jumble of material, from clay-sized particles all the way up to large boulders. In soils that support perennial plants, such as beneath hay fields and woodlands, the roots of trees, shrubs, and even grasses stitch together everything in the soil as a unit. When the ground freezes and expands in the winter and then thaws and settles in the spring, rocks remain fixed in place. However, in cultivated sites that lack perennial roots, rocks can be moved by frozen soils.

This can be pictured as a rock being lifted up through the soil by the frost, creating an empty pocket below it. What most people don't realize is that when the thaw commences in the spring, it moves from the bottom up, not from the top down. Below the frost zone the ground temperature is about 50 degrees Fahrenheit year-round, creating a large reservoir of heat. As the winter abates, the thaw moves upward, collapsing the pocket where the rock originally resided. When the thaw reaches and releases the rock, it can't return to its original position. In this way rocks are slowly ferried to the surface through repeated freeze-and-thaw cycles. When a rock—even a small, fist-sized one—eventually surfaces, a farmer will remove it from the crop field to ease working the soil. If there was a stone wall surrounding the crop field, this is where those small rocks were often left.

As I continued walking along the contour of the slope, I did come to a wall. It was about 2 meters in width, with large rocks framing the edges and small rocks filling the inside. Stone walls built solely around hay fields in New England are generally not very wide and constructed with only large rocks. The wall in front of me was clear evidence that annual plowing had occurred here.

Having figured out that the area holding the cairns had once been a crop field, I was ready to examine the stone structures themselves to see if they meshed with the site's cultivated past. I turned from the wall to walk back toward the center of the site, where I encountered a cluster of cairns. I was immediately struck by their size and the quality of their stonework. These were clearly not merely stone piles. Most of them were rectangular in shape, running lengthwise up- and downslope. The largest ones measured about 7 meters wide by 10 meters long. The external walls were carefully built and then filled with rock in their interiors to create structures that had horizontal flat tops. The downslope walls of the cairns were sometimes close to 3 meters in height, while the upslope walls reached a height of

1 to 2 meters. The cairns' frequency in this once cultivated site, the vast amount of rock that they held, and the nature of their construction made me think that they weren't related to the parcel's past cultivation.

The amount of rock in these cairns and in the surrounding walls was far beyond the volume I had ever seen in a New England crop field of this size, suggesting that much of it may have been imported. The construction of the cairns also made little utilitarian sense. I could imagine that if a crop field generated a large amount of rock, then cairns like these might be made to hold those stones. But the problem with the cairns in this regard was their upslope walls.

If I were going to dispose of rock in this fashion I could see the rationale of building up the downslope and side walls to create a structure into which more rock could be dumped. But why build up the upslope wall so that rock would have to be hauled up and then dumped over a height of 1 to 2 meters? That would have made the work of getting rid of all that rock much more labor-intensive than just dumping it into an expanding cairn.

At this time there is no conclusive evidence to rule out that the cairns were built as a means of removing rock from the crop field, although it seems improbable. However, there is a way to confirm whether or not they are related to the site's past agricultural use. To test the hypothesis that the cairns pre-date cultivation, one of them would need to be taken apart and the ground underneath examined to see if it had an intact soil profile.

If these structures were not there when the area was first cultivated, then the whole parcel would have been plowed, including the ground under each cairn. As such there should be clear evidence that the soil profile had been disturbed under the stone structures. If the soil profile remains intact under a cairn, it would prove that these structures predate the cultivation of the site, and they would have to be assumed to be of Native American origin. But why were they constructed? Are they burial mounds? Do they have calendar significance like the standing stones at Stonehenge? Did they have some ritualistic significance? At this time no one knows.

This account shows how simple, observable evidence within a forest can be used to figure out its past history. It is possible to distinguish former pastures from crop fields, hay fields, and woodlots. It can be inferred if a forest has been subjected to a blowdown in the past and the type of storm responsible for the event. Fire and logging leave clear evidence on the landscape. In addition, all of these events can be roughly dated solely from the visible evidence left on-site.

In the case of the parcel with the cairns, reading the forested landscape has answered some questions about its history, but it has also raised a few more. If the cairns had been found on land that was pillowed and cradled, and a good distance from cultivated land, it would have become immediately clear that they were not related to agricultural activity since farmers rarely transported stone far from its source. Forest forensics is a process that can have importance when trying to reconstruct a landscape's history to pin down an archaeological or cultural story. But reading the forested landscape can also simply be an engaging, mystery-solving activity—one that can help forge a much stronger connection to place.

Many people I have encountered over the past decade who read my first book, *Reading the Forested Landscape,* tell me that they love the idea of interpreting forest histories, but they can't keep all the information straight when out in the woods. It is with these fellow forest investigators in mind that I developed this field guide to reading forest histories.

As a companion to *Reading the Forested Landscape, Forest Forensics* focuses on how to interpret the region's five most common forms of forest disturbance—agricultural abandonment, logging, blowdowns, fire, and ice and snow breakage—while you are out in the woods. In many forests different sections will have dissimilar histories. For example one area might have been a sheep pasture abandoned to grow back to forest in the nineteenth century while an adjacent area may have always been forested and used to supply timber and fuel wood. In such instances it will be important to wander a bit and look for changes in forest age or composition of trees. These changes will often occur at the boundary between sections of forest with different histories. It is along these boundaries where you will often find your most useful evidence—stone walls or boundary trees in this case—to help you interpret a forest's history.

You will also be able to find changes in the composition of tree species when you move from one type of soil or topographic setting to another. In our region it is not unusual to be descending a slope with dry-sited trees like oaks and at the base of the slope enter a stand of red maple growing in saturated soil. In this instance a change in topography gave rise to differing soils and, as a result, two adjacent forest communities developed, with very different compositions.

Forest Forensics is a guide to the entire glaciated region of the northeastern United States and the adjacent provinces of Canada. Very different kinds of forests are found in the region's northern reaches than in its southern portions. This will be true even for forests growing in similar soils or topographic settings. Due to the large geographic scope of this guide, it can't go into changes in forest composition due to soil or topography. Luckily, each state and province has its own guide to the natural forest communities within its boundaries. For example, in my home state, The Nature Conservancy has published a wonderful book, *Wetland, Woodland, Wildland: A Guide to the Natural Communities of Vermont*, by Elizabeth Thompson and Eric Sorenson. *Forest Forensics*, the first field guide to interpret forest disturbance histories, will serve as a companion to state and provincial publications about local natural communities.

Since there are more than 100 pieces of evidence with associated pictures used in this guide, I have arranged it as a dichotomous key to keep the information from becoming jumbled. The key will take you step by step through the evidence in an organized, sequential way until you have unraveled the history of any forest you are examining.

Here's to some exciting reads!

KEY TO READING THE FORESTED LANDSCAPE

Using the Key

This guide's structure is that of a dichotomous key, a tool for discerning, in this case, the history of a piece of land. The key is made up of a series of two-part statements (1A and 1B, 2A and 2B, etc.) wherein the reader chooses the statement that appropriately describes the land that she or he is "reading." Each pair of statements relates to a specific kind of visible evidence. For example, the first pair of statements in this key asks whether the ground is smooth and even or if it has pillows and cradles. Photographs of each feature described are provided in the Plates section following the key so readers can see what smooth and even ground looks like compared to pillowed and cradled ground. Following the key are Evidence sections that are linked to the key numbers; cross-references in the key will direct you to the appropriate sections. These sections—Agriculture, Old Growth and Wind, and Logging and Fire—will provide you with detailed descriptions of how forest features were formed and how they can be used to interpret a site's history. Primers within each Evidence section provide more detailed information, such as the Abandonment Aging Primer, which will help you estimate when a site was abandoned and left to grow back to forest. In this Primer, for example, evidence you'll use to date site abandonment includes weevil-deformed white pines and border trees. Each piece of evidence in the Primer also has associated photographs so you can see exactly what these features look like.

To use the key, read both statements that share the same number. Each statement will guide you to an appropriate photograph in the Plates section. Study the associated photos and then examine your site to figure out which statement best describes it. Once you've determined that, move on to the next set of statements in the hierarchy under the one you have just chosen.

In the Introduction I mentioned my work in the Green Mountain National Forest. Let's now use that site with the cairns as an example of how the key in this guide could be applied to any site.

The key starts by asking you to choose 1A or 1B: Is the ground smooth and even or pillowed and cradled? For the site with the cairns I would pick 1A, smooth and even. Under 1A are choices 2A and 2B: Is the ground level and composed solely of sand or solid clay or is the ground composed of glacial till? In this instance the site with the cairns was sloping and had widely dispersed boulders jutting out of the ground, indicating that it was composed of glacial till, so I would pick 2B. Under 2B are 3A and 3B: Do adjacent stone walls have numerous small, fist-sized stones or do they lack small, fist-sized stones? In this case I would choose 3A since the wall adjacent to the cairns did have lots of small stones. With the choice of 3A, I find that this site was once a crop field.

Since this guide has three sections—the key, the photographic plates, and the evidence—you will find yourself thumbing back and forth between them. However, as you use the guide and become familiar with what the evidence looks like and implies, you will spend less and less time leafing through. In time you may even stop using the guide, having mastered all the evidence within it.

AGRICULTURE

The first section of this key, paired choices numbered 1 to 7, deals with interpreting past agricultural use of currently forested landscapes. Although the majority of the region covered by the key was pasture during the nineteenth century, former hay fields and crop fields will also be encountered. The kinds of evidence used in the key to interpret past agricultural use are the presence or absence of these features: pillows and cradles, stone walls and stone piles, troughs and terraces produced by the annual plowing of crop fields, open-grown trees, and wire fencing (and, if fencing is present, what type). In many cases you may have to go to the borders of the site to find the appropriate evidence, such as stone walls, plow terraces, and plow troughs.

1A The ground is smooth and even, whether or not it is sloping. **See Plate 1A.1.**

- If the ground is not smooth, **go to 1B (p. 21).**

2A The ground is level, without a slope, and is composed solely of sand or solid clay, substrates that often don't create pillows and cradles. **See Evidence (p. 99).**

- **Go to number 4 (p. 20)** to confirm if the site was once a crop field or a hay field.

- **Go to number 6 (p. 21)** to confirm if it was once solely used for pasture.

- **Go to number 8 (p. 22)** to confirm if it has always been forested.

2B The ground is not composed of sand or clay but of glacial till. This is a site that has been plowed in the past for either a hay field or a crop field. Its former pillow and cradle topography was removed by the plowing. **See Evidence (p. 99).**

3A Adjacent stone walls have numerous small, fist-sized stones associated with them, and/or piles of stones—sometimes on top of boulders—grace the site. This site was once a crop field. **See Plates 3A.1–3A.4 and Evidence (pp. 99–100).**

- Go to number 6 (p. 21) to look for subsequent use as pasture.

3B Adjacent walls lack small, fist-sized stones, and no stone piles are present. **See Plate 3B.1.**

4A The site contains plow troughs or bottom plow terraces along its borders. Some glacial tills, outwash sands, and clays don't hold small stones, yet this site was once cultivated for crops. Plow troughs and bottom plow terraces only form through repeated annual plowing. **See Plates 4A.1–4A.4 and Evidence (pp. 100–101).**

- Go to number 6 (p. 21) to look for subsequent use as pasture.

4B Bottom plow terraces and plow troughs are missing, and the soil level is the same on both sides of adjacent walls and fences. This site was once a hayfield that was not plowed frequently enough to form plow troughs and bottom plow terraces. **See Evidence (p. 101).**

1B The ground is not smooth and even, and it has noticeable pillows and cradles or exposed rock that would make the site very difficult to plow or cut hay. **See Plates 1B.1–1B.2 and Evidence (p. 101).**

5A The site has subtle pillow and cradle topography that has been tamped down by the hooves of livestock and/or is surrounded by stone walls or wire fencing. This is a formerly pastured site. **See Plates 5A.1–5A.2 and Evidence (p. 101–102).**

    ● If the pillows and cradles are large, **go to number 5B (p. 22)**.

6A The site has a stone wall but no evidence of other fencing. This pasture was most likely abandoned sometime between 1840 and 1865, the first peak of land abandonment, prior to the mass-production of wire fencing,as people migrated to the Ohio Valley and then farther west.

6B The site has a combination of stone walls and wire fencing, or just wire fencing. This pasture was abandoned after 1874, when wire was first mass-produced.

7A The wire is barbed, the pasture most likely held cows or horses. **See Plate 7A.1 and Evidence (p. 102).**

7B If the wire is smooth mesh, woven wire, indicating the pasture may have held sheep. **See Plate 7B.1 and Evidence (p. 102).**

OLD GROWTH AND WIND

This section covers features indicative of old-growth forests and evidence of wind disturbance. For old-growth forests, coarse bark and deformed canopies are important features to note. Evidence of wind includes live-snapped trees, wind-tipped trees, nurse logs, and the orientation of downed trees or pillows and cradles.

5B The site has large pillows and cradles (5B.1) and may have always been forested. To confirm the land was never cleared for agricultural use, try to find forest-grown trees on the site that germinated prior to 1840, the date that agricultural land first began to be abandoned in the region. **See Plate 5B.1.**

8A The site lacks cut stumps and trees with multiple trunks. **See Plates 8A.1, 8B.1–8B.3, and Evidence (pp. 118 and 126).**

  ● If these features are present, **go to number 8B (p. 24).**

9A Trees of all sizes and ages are present. The largest, oldest trees have coarse, heavily plated bark and deformed canopies. This may be an old-growth stand that was never harvested and has not had a significant stand-altering distur-bance such as a blowdown or fire. **See Plates 9A.1–9A.14 and Evidence (p. 118).**

9B The canopy trees can be estimated at relatively the same age based on similar trunk diameters and similar bark textures within species. If the site was never cleared for agricultural use, look for evidence of a stand-leveling blowdown in either uprooted trees all lying in the same direction (9B.1) or numerous pillows and cradles oriented the same way. **See Plates 9B.1–9B.12 and Evidence (pp. 118–120).**

● If this is the case, **go to number 10, below.**

● If live trees fell in various directions, then the event was an ice storm, snowstorm, or a tornado. If it was a tornado, the area impacted would be limited in size, whereas snow and ice damage will be regionally widespread.

10A The winds were from the west; the event was most likely a thunderstorm microburst. **See Evidence (p. 121).**

10B The winds are from the southeast; the event was most likely a hurricane. Winds from the northeast are either a hurricane or, if within 75 miles of the Atlantic coastline, a nor'easter. Winds from the north are often the result of high-pressure gales.

LOGGING AND FIRE

In this section, important evidence of logging includes stumps without an associated downed trunk, multiple-trunked trees, and sets of opposing basal scars. For fire, the important evidence is uphill basal scars, multiple-trunked trees that retain their original dead trunks, rot-resistant snags, and the presence of charcoal.

8B The site has cut stumps or multiple-trunked trees. **See Plates 8B.1-8B.3 and Evidence (p. 126)**.

11A If the site contains stumps with flat tops or stumps that don't have an associated log from deadfall, then the site has been logged. **See Evidence (p. 126)**.

● See the Stump Decay Primer (p. 136) to identify the species and estimate the age of the stumps.

11B The site has no stumps other than those from deadfall trees, but there are multiple-trunked trees present.

12A The original trunks of the multiple-trunked trees are larger than 18 inches in diameter at ground level. Look for sets of opposing basal scars to confirm logging. **See Plates 12A.1– 12A.3 and Evidence (pp. 126–127).**

12B The original trunks were less than 18 inches in diameter at ground level, look for opposing basal scars to confirm logging or uphill basal scars to confirm fire. If each multiple-trunked tree has a standing snag in the middle of it, an associated deadfall trunk on the ground, or if the original trunk was just a few inches in diameter, then the disturbance was a fire (unless the multiple-trunked trees are American chestnuts). **See Plates 12B.1–12B.4 and Evidence (pp. 126–128).**

PLATES

1A.1 Smooth, even ground

1B.1 Pillowed and cradled ground

1B.2 Rocky ground

3A.1 Stone wall with small stones throughout

3A.2 Stone wall with small rocks filling the middle

3A.3 Rock pile

3A.4 Rock pile on a boulder

3B.1 Stone wall with only large rocks

4A.1 Bottom plow terrace

4A.2 Plow trough adjacent to stone wall

4A.3 Higher soil level on the left side of stone wall
due to annual plowing

4A.4 Road cut

5A.1 Subtly pillowed and cradled ground

5A.2 Pasture tree

5B.1 Large pillow and cradle

7A.1 Barbed wire on pasture side of post

7B.1 Smooth mesh wire fencing

8A.1 Uncut stump and associated deadfall trunk

8B.1 Cut stump with flat top

8B.2 Cut stump with no associated deadfall trunk

8B.3 Multiple-trunked red oak

9A.1 100-year-old black birch

9A.2 Old-growth black birch

9A.3 100-year-old hemlock

9A.4 Old-growth hemlock

9A.5 100-year-old red oak

9A.6 Old-growth red oak

9A.7 100-year-old sugar maple

9A.8 Old-growth sugar maple

9A.9 100-year-old white pine

9A.10 Old-growth white pine

9A.11 100-year-old yellow birch

9A.12 Old-growth yellow birch

9A.13 Old-growth black gum

9A.14 Deformed canopy of a black gum

9B.1 Blown-down trees all lying in the same direction

9B.2 Tip-up—the roots and excavated earth of
a downed live tree

9B.3 Uprooted deadfall oak—not an indicator of a blowdown, snow, or ice event

9B.4 Deadfall snap, not an indicator of a blowdown, snow, or ice event

9B.5 Live-snapped tree from wind or from snow-
or ice-loading

9B.6 Wind-tipped hemlock

9B.7 Wind-tipped hardwood with lowest branch replacing
the original trunk

9B.8 Tree bent over by weight, with lowest branch replacing the original trunk

9B.9 White pine nurse log with young hemlocks growing on it

9B.10 Trees growing in line with aboveground roots stretching between them—evidence of a nurse log

9B.11 Stilt-rooted black birch on a pillow

9B.12 Paper birch growing on a pillow

11A.3 Uncut stump and associated deadfall trunk

12A.1 How to estimate the diameter of the original trunk of a multiple-trunked tree—7 inches at ground level in this case.

12A.2 Opposing basal scars

12A.3 Basal scar on a hemlock with annual growth lines on
the bark of the callus

12B.1 Uphill-facing basal fire scars

12B.2 Multiple-trunked tree with associated deadfall trunk

12B.3 Heat-killed snag with multiple stump-sprouts

12B.4 American chestnut snag with multiple stump-sprouts

EVIDENCE

EVIDENCE OF AGRICULTURE

CROP FIELDS AND HAY FIELDS

2A. When live trees are toppled by wind or snow- or by ice-loading, their roots rip out of the ground, excavating a pit or cradle. As the tipped-up roots decay, they drop the earth they excavated, creating a mound or pillow adjacent to the cradle. When this occurs on dry, sandy substrates, roots often rip out of the ground without excavating a cradle. On clay plains, roots only grow along the surface, and when a tree is toppled the roots excavate no earth. Sites such as these often don't develop distinct pillow and cradle topography and are naturally smooth and even, despite their history of toppled trees.

2B. Large pillows and cradles can still be observed almost a millennium after the event that dropped the trees, so a lack of pillows and cradles means the ground was once plowed. On sites such as these there may be a few small pillows and cradles, usually all in the same orientation, from a blowdown within a young forest grown up after abandonment of the site. To get pillows and cradles on many different orientations usually takes centuries.

3A. Crop fields were plowed each year prior to planting seeds; this activity prevented perennial roots of trees, shrubs, and grasses from taking hold. Sites without perennial roots allow rocks to surface each spring. As the ground freezes and expands in the winter, rocks are ferried upward, leaving a hollow below them. Contrary to popular opinion, at the end of the winter the ground begins to thaw from the bottom up, not the top down. Below the frost zone the earth has a consistent temperature around 50–55 degrees F. As the winter abates, the thaw creeps upward, collapsing the hollow beneath each rock. When the rock is released by thaw, it can't drop back down to its original position. In this way, over the course of years rocks are slowly carried to the surface, where they have to be removed since they get in the way of working the soil. Rocks don't surface in forests or hay fields since the perennial roots of trees, shrubs, and grasses lock each rock into place so that the ground freezes and thaws as a unit. Only cultivated sites generate small rocks each year.

3A. and **4A**. Prior to the mid-1800s all northeastern farms grew their own grains such as wheat, barley, rye, and flax; this was a very labor-intensive farming activity. Once rail developed in the northeast during the mid-1800s and grain could then be easily shipped from the South or Midwest, it was no longer necessary for New Englanders to cultivate grains. As a result, many crop fields were converted into hay fields or pastures to support the rise in market dairy farms that could also utilize the new rail system to ship dairy products into urban centers.

4A. To ease the burden on farmer and animal, crop fields were plowed so that the plow furrow was turned downslope. With each plowing, soil migrated downhill, and where the plowing stopped a bottom plow terrace (4A.1) developed. This feature juts *out from* the slope, in contrast to a road cut (4A.4) that, as its name suggests, cuts *into* the slope.

Since the farmer couldn't plow right up to a stone wall, plow troughs (4A.2) developed adjacent to stone walls; the bottom of the trough indicates the original, lower level of the unplowed ground next to the plowed field.

In some cases annual plowing pushed the soil right up to a stone wall. Where this happened the soil level on the plowed side of the wall is noticeably higher than the other side (4A.3).

4B. Like cultivated sites, hay fields had to be plowed to remove pillow and cradle topography that would make scything hay difficult. However, hay fields were only plowed a few times over the course of their use to prepare them, not every year as was the case with crop fields. So hay fields didn't develop plow terraces or troughs due to limited movement of soil.

PASTURE

1B. When live trees are toppled by wind or by snow- or ice-loading their roots rip out of the ground, excavating a pit or cradle. As the tipped-up roots decay they drop the earth they excavated, creating a mound or pillow adjacent to the cradle (1B.1, pp. 40–41). Large pillows and cradles can be observed almost a millennium after the event that dropped the trees.

5A. The hooves of livestock can tramp down and erode pillow and cradle topography, but they usually can't remove all evidence of it (5A.1). Pasture trees may also be present (5A.2). These are trees that grew by themselves in full sunlight and put their energy into growing outward, with large low branches, rather than racing upward in the canopy of a forest. They are always found growing in the midst of a former pasture, not on a fence line. These trees were intentionally left to provide shade for livestock on hot summer afternoons. They would not have been left in a cultivated site or in a hay field where their presence would reduce the productivity of those areas.

7A. If the wire was attached to small trees or fence posts, generally less than 4 inches in diameter, the side of the tree or post where the wire is attached is the pastured side of the fence (7A.1). Wire was strung in this manner so that if the livestock leaned into the fence they would be pushing the wire into the tree or post and not away from it where they could detach it. On larger trees that could accept big nails, wire could be strung on any side that was most convenient.

7B. With their heavy fleece, sheep can't feel the barbs on barbed wire and can get tangled in fencing and become injured. For this reason, smooth wire mesh was preferred for sheep (7B.1).

Abandonment Aging Primer

WEEVIL-DEFORMED PINES

To estimate the date your forest was abandoned as agricultural land, look for weevil-damaged white pines. The white pine weevil is a native beetle that lays its eggs in the upright terminal shoot at the top of white pine trees. But not any terminal shoot will do. The pine generally needs to be between 5 and 30 feet in height and growing in full sunlight. This will create a robust terminal shoot that is as thick as a finger, making it suitable forage for the white pine weevil larvae. When they hatch, the larvae drill into and eat the terminal shoot, killing it (A.1, p. 104). This causes the branches from the limb whorl (lateral branches) directly below the terminal shoot to begin growing upward in an effort to replace the terminal shoot. Generally if three or more limbs of a white pine do this, the tree grew in the open by itself and may have been a pasture tree (A.2, p. 105). If only two limbs replaced the terminal shoot, these trees would be the first cohort of pines to invade the site just after abandonment; they would have had to compete for sun in their race to the canopy, limiting the number of limbs (A.3, p. 106).

To age the pines, simply count the number of limb whorls, or tiers of branches, since pines grow only one limb whorl each year. If white pines are not present, see the Tree-Aging Primer on page 123 to age the largest forest-grown canopy trees.

A.1 Leader of a young white pine killed by
the white pine weevil

A.2 Weevil-damaged white pine with numerous
upward-arching limbs

A.3 Weevil-damaged white pines with just two upward-arching limbs

PASTURE SHRUBS

Overgrazed pastures abandoned after 1940 may have pasture shrubs, most notably robust populations of common juniper (A.4, pp. 108–109) or multiflora rose. Both species are slow-growing during their first few years and are intolerant of being shaded (A.7, p. 114), so they can only establish on a site where herbaceous growth is limited. This occurs in pastures where livestock will graze the herbaceous plants around the unpalatable juniper and multiflora rose, giving these plants the chance to establish. However, in abandoned hay fields or on cultivated sites, herbaceous plants grow more quickly than the young shrubs, covering them and killing them. Healthy populations of common juniper can also be found in the crevices of bedrock outcroppings (A.5, pp. 110–111) and in dry, sandy soils where herbaceous growth is limited but carpets of drought tolerant hair-cap moss or star moss will form (A.6, pp. 112–113). On these sites, other evidence will need to be found to confirm former pasture. Common juniper's close relative, eastern red cedar, frequently establishes itself on abandoned agricultural sites, but since it grows upright it can also establish in hay fields and on cultivated sites. So the presence of eastern red cedar alone doesn't define the previous agricultural land use.

A.4 Common juniper in an overgrazed pasture

A.5 Common juniper on a rock outcropping

A.6 Common juniper in a mat of moss

A.7 Branches of a dead common juniper killed by shading

BORDER TREES

To determine if the land on one side of a fence line was abandoned prior to the other side, look at the growth form of the trees along the fence line. If one side of the trees has large, low-growing limbs (A.8, p. 116) or rounded knobs from limbs that have died and healed over (A.9, p. 117), this side of the trees grew in the open. Thus you can infer that this side of the trees and fence line was abandoned more recently.

A.8 Border tree with large low branches growing on one side

A.9 Border tree with large, low, healed-over limb knobs
on one side

EVIDENCE OF OLD GROWTH AND WIND

8A. Recently cut stumps have flat tops (8B.1). Decayed stumps will lose their flat tops but can be identified as being cut if there is no associated trunk on the ground near them (8B.2). Stumps created from deadfall will usually have an associated trunk on the ground (8A.1).

9A. Within a species, all individual trees produce the same thickness of bark each year. However, the amount of wood they produce is variable based on growing conditions or age. Compare the bark and thickness of 100-year-old trees with their old-growth counterparts in the accompanying photographs (9A.1–9A.14). The 100-year-old trees have smoother bark, as the first 100 years of a tree's growth is when they produce their thickest annual growth rings. Old trees produce very small annual growth rings, often from 15–30 rings in the outermost inch of wood. As a result of this slow growth of wood, the bark isn't stretched by increasing girth of the tree and builds up into coarse plates. Old-growth birch, maple, beech, and red oak can reach over 300 years of age. Old-growth white oak, white pine, and hemlock can reach over 400 years of age. Old-growth black gum can reach over 600 years of age.

9B. When live trees are toppled by wind or by snow- or ice-loading, their roots rip out of the ground, excavating a pit or cradle (9B.2). As the tipped-up roots decay, they drop the earth they excavated, creating a mound or pillow adjacent to the cradle. Deadfall snags (standing dead trees that fall over) don't create pillows and cradles when they topple. Their roots rot to the point where the trunks just fall over, as is commonly seen in oaks (9B.3) Alternatively, their trunks snap off near ground level, where decay occurs more readily due to higher levels of moisture in the wood of that part of the trunk (9B.4). Live trees that are snapped by wind or snow- or ice-loading often break at mid-trunk height (9B.5). The exception to this is paper birch, the bark of which is impervious to moisture movement from the inside to the outside of the tree; this causes rot to occur at equal rates throughout the tree. Thus, dead paper birch trees can snap at any rotten point along their trunks.

Wind often causes young trees to be tipped at an angle rather than blown down completely. In this scenario, the tops of tipped, young conifers will grow toward the light, usually into the canopy gap or opening created by their tipping. Eventually the tops of these trees will grow vertically again, creating bowed trunks and straight tops (9B.6). The middle of the bow represents the height of the tree when it was tipped. By comparison, hardwoods that are tipped when young grow to have lower trunks often leaning at a 45-degree angle and upper trunks formed from the lowest living limb that grows straight up from this bend toward the canopy gap. This vigorously growing vertical limb will often shade and kill the remainder of the original trunk (9B.7). Trees bent by the weight of other falling trees, snow, or ice have trunks that bend over toward the ground before their lowest living limb grows upward into the canopy gap. (9B.8).

Toppled white pine or spruce trees may serve as nurse

logs (9B.9). These species slowly decay from the outside in and, after 20 years of decay, drop their bark on the ground. Moss can then cover the downed trunks in a few years, and the mat it creates is a great germination site for small-seeded, shade-tolerant trees like hemlock, black birch, yellow birch, balsam fir, and spruce. After the nurse log decays, it will leave a series of trees growing in a straight line with their aboveground, horizontal roots tying the trees together (9B.10).

To age a wind event where the downed trees have rotted away, look for these kinds of evidence:

• Trees with stilt-like roots growing on pillows (9B.11). The roots will fan out like a river delta. These trees germinated in the soil-caked roots of the downed tree and grew down into the deeper soil of the pillow.

• Small-seeded, shade-intolerant trees like paper birch or aspen growing on the pillows (9B.12). These trees germinated just after the pillow formed, while there was still bare soil. After leaf litter covers the pillow, the small seeds of these trees cannot successfully penetrate to the soil below to establish themselves.

In either case, estimate the age of the tree (see the Tree-Aging Primer on page 123) and add approximately 15–25 years for a stilt-rooted tree or 30–40 years for a small-seeded, shade-intolerant tree to establish.

10A. To determine wind direction, stand on the pillow and look over the cradle and you will be looking into the direction the wind came from. But be aware that in certain terrain, such as narrow valleys, strong winds can be directed in ways that don't conform to the usual paths for storm-generated, stand-leveling winds.

T.1 Two white pines—the older, right-hand tree has a much coarser bark texture

Tree-Aging Primer

Rough estimates of tree age can be made based on diameter and bark texture. For canopy trees growing on moderate sites (in terms of moisture and nutrient levels), at 1 foot in diameter they will be about 50 years of age and at 2 feet, about 100 years of age. But there are many exceptions to this rule, listed below:

• Canopy-suppressed trees or trees growing on dry, nutrient-poor sites will grow more slowly and be older at the above diameters.

• Open-grown trees or trees growing on moist, nutrient-rich sites will grow faster and be younger at the above diameters.

• Upland trees such as tulip tree, white pine, red oak, and white ash grow faster than other species, so they will be younger at the above diameters.

• Alluvial flood plain species such as silver maple, sycamore, eastern cottonwood, and American elm grow quite fast and are often half the age at the above diameters.

• Multiple-trunked trees will be older at the above diameters since the root system is supporting a number of trunks. The greater the number of trunks, the slower that each puts on trunk diameter. By calculating the basal area of each of the trunks and combining them, one can calculate the basal area of a single combined trunk to estimate when the cutting of the original tree occurred. As an example, imagine a tree with three trunks each 8 inches in diameter. Using the formula, *area=3.14 x radius squared*, each trunk would have a basal area of 50 square inches (3.14 x 16), so all three trunks combined would have a total of 150 square inches of basal area. Reversing the formula, 150 square inches gives a radius of 7 inches or a trunk diameter of 14 inches if the three trunks were merged. A 14-inch-diameter tree is roughly equivalent to 60 years, which dates the time of cutting of this tree.

Within a species, individual trees produce the same thickness of bark each year. However, the amount of wood they produce is variable based on growing conditions or age. Fast-growing trees that lay down wide annual growth rings will stretch their bark, giving it a less rough appearance, while on slow-growing trees the bark can build up to a very rough appearance (T.1, p. 122).

If the trunk of the tree is leaning, you should examine the portion of the trunk that faces the ground. This is where you will find the representative bark of the tree. On many species of trees such as white oak, ash, white pine, hemlock, maple, birch, black gum, and others supporting bark ridges, the bark on skyward facing portions of the trunk can capture wet snow. When the wet snow freezes and expands, it can exfoliate the bark, making it appear less rough than is typical of the species (T.2). Whenever estimating tree age by diameter, also examine the bark texture to see if it is rougher or smoother than might be expected for the tree's size and then adjust your estimate of age either up or down.

T.2 Leaning old growth black gum—coarse bark on ground-facing side (right), smoother bark on sky-facing side (left)

EVIDENCE OF LOGGING AND FIRE

8A, **8B**, and **11A**. Stumps created from deadfall will usually have an associated trunk on the ground (8A.1). Recently cut stumps have flat tops (8B.1). Decayed stumps will lose their flat tops but can be identified as being cut if there is no associated trunk on the ground near them (8B.2). Multiple-trunked trees are also evidence of logging (8B.3).

12A. and **12B**. Many hardwood trees have the ability to regenerate by stump-sprouting after being cut or being killed by the heat of a fire. Latent buds under the bark at ground level are stimulated by stress, such as cutting, and the roots of these still-living plants send nutrients to foster the growth of these buds. Several sprouts will grow initially, with usually just two or three surviving as the tree's new trunks. Since the stump sprouts arise near ground level around the base of a tree, it is possible to estimate the diameter of the original trunk prior to stump-sprouting. To do so, run your hands down the middle of the two outermost trunks of the multiple-trunked tree to ground level. Then bring your hands in toward each other so that only about the inner one-third of the diameter of each trunk lies between your hands. The distance between your hands represents an estimate of the diameter at ground level of the tree's original trunk (12A.1). The reason for bringing your hands together is that the center, or pith, of the trunks of multiple-trunked trees are not in the middle of each trunk, but rather approximately one-third of the total diameter from the inner side. Since these stump-sprouted trees have little room to grow branches on the inside of their trunks because of the close spacing, they lay down more wood on the outside.

You may suspect that the original trunks of these stump-sprouted trees were killed by fire. Generally northeastern trees greater than 18 inches in diameter often survive a blaze due to their thicker bark and the greater thermal mass of their wood that, in combination, resist the damaging heat of a fire. Trees of this size were more likely removed by logging. To confirm that this is the case, try to find areas where logs may have been pulled upslope or downslope from each multiple-trunked tree or along skid roads. Then look for sets of opposing basal scars (12A.2). These scars occur where logs, as they were dragged, hit the trunks of neighboring trees, removing their bark and creating scars that face each other. If these scars occur on hemlock, closely examine the callus wood growing over the scar (12A.3). Since an annual growth line is produced each year on the bark of a hemlock callus, a count of the annual growth lines will equal the number of years since the logging.

12B. On a slope, fires usually generate uphill basal scars (12B.1). These form due to the creation of fuel pockets on the uphill side of a tree's trunk. Over time, leaf litter, branches, and even downed logs are pulled downhill by gravity. Each standing tree trunk acts like a dam to this movement, so pockets of fuel build up on the uphill side of a tree while the downhill side often has little fuel around it. When the fire reaches such a tree it burns longer on the uphill side, killing the cambial tissue under the bark. Months after a fire, the bark falls off of this side of the tree, creating an uphill-facing basal scar that is often triangular in shape.

Multiple-trunked trees that have a central standing snag (12B.3) or a deadfall trunk on the ground (12B.2) that was the original trunk were not logged. If these trees are not American chestnut—a species that stump-sprouts after its trunk is killed by an exotic fungus (12B.4)—then they were most likely heat-killed by a fire.

Other Evidence of Fire Primer

Other evidence of fire includes age discontinuities in forests with trees older than 150 years, rot-resistant standing pine or spruce snags, and charcoal—often the least visible evidence of fire.

AGE DISCONTINUITY

When forests over 150 years of age are subjected to fire, the large old trees often survive the blaze due to their thicker bark and the greater thermal mass of their wood that, in combination, resist the damaging heat of a fire. Small- and medium-sized trees are often killed and eventually replaced by an even-aged, younger cohort of trees that colonize after the fire. The result is a forest populated with just two age classes—the larger, older, fire-resistant trees and the smaller, young, post-fire cohort (F.1, pp. 130). In younger forests with trees 100 years old or less, this age discontinuity can happen naturally, since it may take many decades before understory trees can establish under the dense, young canopy. As a forest develops gaps in its canopy, understory trees filling these gaps grow more vigorously. This eventually creates a medium-sized cohort; young saplings will continue to populate the understory and form the next age class.

ROT-RESISTANT SNAGS

Numerous rot-resistant standing pine or spruce snags in the canopy are good evidence of fire. Since these trees die quickly and shed their bark following a fire, they are not often attacked by bark beetles and borers that in live trees

F.1 Age discontinuity

compromise the outer sapwood, making it rot-prone. As a result, these conifer snags are quite rot-resistant and can persist as standing snags for many decades (F.2, p. 132). Their trunks are often free of fungi and look smooth and gray in appearance. The presence of a small cluster of these pine or spruce snags may be due to a lightning strike. To confirm this, see if you can find vertical scars spiraling up the trees along the wood grain (F.3, p. 133).

CHARCOAL

Charcoal is often hard to find in older burned sites in the northeast since the only wood that burns here is already dead at the time of the fire. Our region's living trees rarely burn, and the singed portions of their bark are often shed within a few years. Charcoal will most readily be found on basal scars that were already present prior to a fire and on snags or deadfall (F.4, p. 134). Be sure you are observing charcoal and not charcoal mat fungus that naturally covers the wood of maple, beech, and elm in late stages of decay. Charcoal mat fungus (F.5, pp. 135) has a smooth surface that often looks like it has been sculpted with a wood gouge, not broken into a blocky pattern like charcoal. Also, charcoal mat fungus won't rub off on your fingers as does charcoal.

FIRE-PRONE COMMUNITIES

Fire-prone sites in the northeast support drought-tolerant, fire-adapted trees and shrubs such as pitch pine, jack pine, red pine, bear oak, chestnut oak, white oak, low-bush blueberry, and black huckleberry.

F.2 Rot-resistant, heat-killed pine snag

F.3 Spiraling lightning scar

F.4 Charcoal on dead snag

F.5 Charcoal mat fungus on a sugar maple branch

Stump Decay Primer

Stumps can be divided into four groups based on decay patterns. These include coniferous stumps, rot-resistant hardwood stumps, rot-prone hardwood stumps, and hardwood stumps that are intermediate in their decay rates. The descriptions given below are for stumps that were sound, meaning that they had no rot when they were cut. Although this primer focuses on stumps, the information is applicable to trunks of trees as well, as they will decay in the same fashion as their stumps. Site conditions and stump size can strongly influence decay rates. Small stumps and those on moist sites decay more quickly. Large stumps and those on dry sites decay more slowly. The descriptions below are for stumps on moderate sites that are intermediate in size—about 2 feet in diameter at the time of cutting. Since many trees when they are cut do have rot within them that alters decay patterns and rates, care must be taken when identifying and aging stumps or downed trees.

CONIFEROUS STUMPS

All conifers native to the region—with the exception of cedars—have wood that rots from the outside in. Cedars naturally rot from the inside out, creating stumps with hollow centers and the most intact wood on the outside. Many coniferous stumps can become coated with moss as they age. To confirm a stump is coniferous, other than a cedar, just probe the side of the stump with a finger. If your finger first penetrates punky (soft, crumbling) wood before hitting a harder center on a number of tries, you have a conifer.

S.1 Exposed limb whorl within a white pine stump—
about 35 years of decay

■ EASTERN WHITE PINE

Our most common conifer to be logged in the region is eastern white pine. Generally white pine stumps will drop their bark within 25 years after cutting. If the tree grew with ample light when it was young, limb whorls should be present on the outside of the stump. After about 35 years of decay, the stump will rot, often exposing the more decay-resistant limb whorl within it (S.1, p. 137). After more than 70 years, all that will be left of the stump is the limb whorl and some fins of wood associated with each limb of the whorl (S.2).

S.2 Fin wood associated with the limb whorl of a white pine stump—about 70 years of decay

■ EASTERN HEMLOCK

Our next most common conifer to be logged is eastern hemlock. Like white pine it has wood that decays from the outside in, and the wood is usually completely gone in about 50 years. However, unlike white pine, hemlock does not have limb whorls, but it does have very persistent, rot-resistant bark that can leave perfectly intact bark rings after the wood of the stump has decayed away (S.3). The only other tree in the region to create persistent bark rings is big-toothed aspen (S.4, p. 140). Since hemlock trees have a strong

S.3 Hemlock bark ring—about 40 years of decay

propensity to root-graft with neighboring hemlocks, after being cut many hemlock stumps continue to grow. The bark of the callus wood of these stumps lays down annual growth lines (S.5). Counting the number of these annual growth lines until you intersect the original bark will tell you when the tree was cut. This technique can also be used to age hemlock basal scars from logging or fire events up to the point when the basal scar completely heals over.

S.4 Bigtooth aspen bark ring—the tree was cut down by a beaver

■ SPRUCE

Since species of spruce decay very much like white pine after dropping their bark, the best way to determine the species of the stump is by examining surrounding trees in the forest.

■ BALSAM FIR

Balsam fir decays like white pine but more quickly, and unlike pine and spruce, it lacks fin wood.

S.5 Cut hemlock with callus growth from root grafting

■ NURSE STUMPS

Both white pine and spruce stumps can serve as nurse sites. About a decade after cutting, the wood just inside the bark on the top of these stumps decays to the point where it can support a ring of moss. The moss provides a good germination site for small-seeded, shade-tolerant trees like hemlock, spruce, yellow birch, black birch, and balsam fir. The roots of these trees grow down just inside the bark of the stump, often wrapping around it. Once the stump decays away, what is left is a stilt-rooted tree, whose roots grow in a semicircular pattern that approximates the diameter of the original stump. If trees have some interior decay when cut, tree seedlings can germinate in the center of a nurse stump. In this instance their roots will grow over the top of the stump and then down its sides (S.6).

S.6 Young hemlock on a white pine nurse stump

S.7 Sugar maple stump covered in charcoal mat fungus

ROT-PRONE HARDWOOD STUMPS

Most hardwoods, such as maple, beech, birch, elm, and aspen, have wood that rots uniformly and quickly. These stumps, even on large specimens, are usually completely decayed within 30–40 years. In late stages of decay, the wood of maple, elm, and beech trees become coated in charcoal mat fungus, helping to identify these groups (S.7). Charcoal mat fungus appears black like charcoal, but it has a smooth surface, unlike charcoal's blocky pattern; also, charcoal mat fungus won't rub off on your fingers. If the stumps in your forest are coated in charcoal mat fungus, examine the remaining surrounding trees and you may be able to guess what species were cut.

INTERMEDIATE HARDWOOD STUMPS

These include members of the red oak group, hickory, ash, and black cherry. These species have wood that doesn't decay in any particular pattern, but their stumps will persist for about 75 years, placing them in between rot-prone and rot-resistant hardwood species.

ROT-RESISTANT HARDWOOD STUMPS

While most hardwood species have stumps that rot uniformly and quite quickly, usually decaying completely within 30–40 years, a few species have rot-resistant stumps that can persist longer than a century.

■ WHITE OAK GROUP (INCLUDES NORTHERN WHITE OAK, SWAMP WHITE OAK, BUR OAK, CHESTNUT OAK)

The oaks are divided into two subgroups: the red oak group, with leaves that have pointed leaf lobes, and the white oak group, the species featuring leaves with rounded lobes. The outer heartwood of the trees of white oak species is especially decay resistant, lasting more than a century, while the center, or inner heartwood, can begin to decay in 50 years.

S.8 Cut oak stump showing white ray lines

By this time, the outer wood of the stump starts to develop vertical fissures that get bigger as the stump ages. Hollowed-out white oak stumps can be identified by their visible ray lines that run from the outside of the stump toward the center, cutting across the annual growth lines (S.8). These ray lines can also be seen as vertical lines when carving through the bark into the outer wood of an oak trunk (S.9). Oaks are the only trees that have ray lines visible to the naked eye.

S.9 Carved oak trunk showing parallel ray lines

S.10 Hollowed-out American chestnut stump

■ AMERICAN CHESTNUT

The stumps of American chestnut (S.10) look very much like white oak and decay at similar rates. However, chestnuts lack vertical ray lines. To confirm you have a chestnut, carve into the outer wood. Since chestnut has ring-porous wood, the ring-porous section of an annual growth ring can look like ray lines, but once beyond this section all vertical lines disappear (S.11). Continue carving, and if you hit a depth without vertical lines, you have a chestnut tree.

S.11 Carved American chestnut trunk showing no ray lines

S.12 Hollowed-out black locust stump with black fungus

■ BLACK LOCUST

The stumps of black locust decay in a way similar to white oak and chestnut, but unlike these trees, black locust tends to develop a thin layer of black fungus on its outer wood in late stages of decay (S.12). Often site conditions can be used to distinguish black locust stumps from white oak and chestnut stumps. Black locust does well on nutrient-rich, moist soils, whereas white oak and chestnut tend to favor poorer, drier sites. The exceptions to this are swamp white oak and bur oak that thrive in moist sites.

QUICK-REFERENCE CHARTS

Agricultural Abandonment Evidence

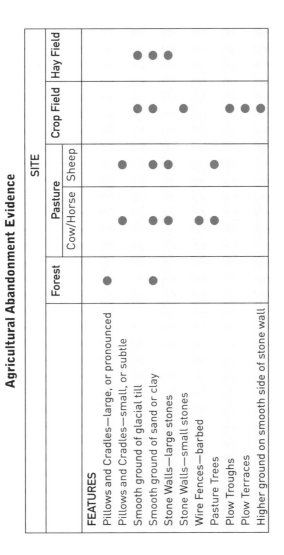

| FEATURES | SITE | | | | |
---	Forest	Pasture Cow/Horse	Pasture Sheep	Crop Field	Hay Field
Pillows and Cradles—large, or pronounced	●				
Pillows and Cradles—small, or subtle	●				
Smooth ground of glacial till		●	●	●	●
Smooth ground of sand or clay		●	●	●	●
Stone Walls—large stones		●	●		●
Stone Walls—small stones				●	
Wire Fences—barbed		●			
Pasture Trees		●	●		
Plow Troughs				●	
Plow Terraces				●	
Higher ground on smooth side of stone wall				●	

Common Plant Species of Abandoned Agricultural Land

	SITE		
	Pasture	Crop Field	Hay Field
SPECIES			
Common juniper	●		
Multiflora rose	●		
Eastern red cedar	●	●	●

Old Growth and Disturbance Characteristics of Northeastern Forests

	DISTURBANCE				
	Old Growth	Wind	Snow or Ice	Logging	Fire
FEATURE					
Pillows and cradles	●	●	●		
Large trees	●				
Coarse bark	●				
Trees—all sizes and ages	●				
Trees—same size and ages		●		●	●
Deformed canopies	●		●		
Cut stumps, no deadfall				●	
Stumps with deadfall					●
Dead standing snags					●
Live-snapped trees		●	●		
Weight-bent trees		●	●		
Tipped trees		●			
Nurse logs		●	●		
Multiple-trunked trees				●	●
Uphill basal scars					●
Opposing basal scars				●	
Charcoal					●

GLOSSARY

age discontinuity—forests older than 150 years that lack medium-sized trees due to fire

bark rings—rings of hemlock or big-toothed aspen bark that persist long after the wood of its stump has decayed away

basal area—the area of the cross-section of a tree, normally taken at breast height (4.5 feet) and used in forestry to estimate tree and stand volume. In the case of forest forensics, the measurement is used to determine the diameter of a **multiple-trunked tree**

basal scars—scars at the base of tree trunks created by the removal of bark from fire or some form of impact, such as from logging equipment

blowdown—an area of live trees uprooted and toppled by wind

border trees—trees that grow on the border of open or once open agricultural plots

bottom plow terrace—a terrace that juts out from a slope at the bottom of a crop field where soil was deposited after numerous annual plowings

callus—the wood and bark that grow over a wound in the trunk or branch of a tree

cambium—the living tissue just under the bark of a tree that separates the xylem and phloem, the cells that transport water, nutrients, and carbohydrates

canopy gap—an opening in the canopy formed by the removal of one or more trees

canopy-suppressed trees—shaded, slow-growing trees under the canopy of a forest

charcoal mat fungus—a black fungus that covers the wood of beech, elm, and maple in late stages of decay

cohort—trees of the same age within a forest

conifers—needle- and cone-bearing trees

deadfall—standing dead trees that fall to the ground

deadfall snap—standing dead trees whose trunks snap off near ground level

fin wood—decay-resistant wood associated with the limbs of white pine and spruce trees

forest-grown trees—trees that grew up into the canopy of a forest and consequently have lower trunks with few or no limbs

fuel pocket—bunches of leaves, sticks, limbs, and even logs that build up on the uphill side of a tree trunk on a slope

glacial till—a jumble of material—from fine, clay-sized particles up to large rocks—that was dropped in place by a melting glacier

hardwoods—broad-leaved, deciduous trees

heartwood—the interior, dead wood of a tree that doesn't carry sap

limb whorls—in pines, spruce, and fir, the clusters of three or more branches that grow around the trunk at the same height; these trees grow one limb whorl each year

live-snapped trees—trees whose trunks break at mid-height due to wind or snow- or ice-loading

multiple-trunked trees—trees that have more than one trunk growing from their root system; also known as coppiced trees

nurse logs—downed trunks of pine or spruce on which small-seeded, shade-tolerant trees like black birch, yellow birch, hemlock, and spruce grow

nurse stumps—stumps of pine or spruce on which small-seeded, shade-tolerant trees like black birch, yellow birch, hemlock, and spruce grow

old-growth—forests that have trees of all ages, canopy trees at maximum age for their species, and no evidence of any stand-altering disturbance

open-grown trees—trees that grew by themselves in a pasture or field, or on a fence line or border; they can be identified by their large, wide-spreading, low-growing limbs

opposing basal scars—scars that face each other at the base of adjacent trees; these are created by the dragging of logs during a logging operation

outwash sands—sand deposited by glacial-meltwater rivers as their velocity slowed

pasture shrubs—shrubs such as common juniper and multiflora rose that invade overgrazed pastures

pasture trees—open-grown trees that do not lie on a fence line or border but grew in the midst of a pasture

perennial—any plant that lives longer than two years

pillows and cradles—features on the ground of a forest created by the uprooting and subsequent decay of live trees; also known as **pits and mounds**

plow trough—a feature of crop fields that develops near stone walls because plows were unable to work these margins of the fields due to the proximity to the wall; the trough is the level of original unplowed ground

ray lines—clusters of cells that run from the center of a tree's trunk to the outside and are responsible for horizontal movement of sap within the vascular tissue of a tree; rays are only visible to the naked eye in oak trees

ring-porous wood—the wood of certain trees, such as American chestnut and ash, which forms large cells early in the growing season and smaller cells later in the season; this is visible in the annual growth rings when the tree is cut; when the wood is carved into, the cells are similar in appearance to ray lines

road cut—a feature of a forest created by clearing the vegetation along a slope and grading it level to make it passable for vehicles, such as logging or farm equipment

root graft—roots of neighboring trees, usually growing within 15 feet of each other, that graft on to each other; this is common in hemlock trees

sapwood—the living portion of the outer wood of a tree; this includes the xylem, phloem, and cambium and is responsible for transporting sap and nutrients

skid roads—forest roads used to drag logs out of the woods during a logging operation

shade-tolerant—plants that can survive in shady environments

snag—a standing dead tree

soil profile—the naturally occurring arrangement of distinct layers known as horizons that form in soils which have been free from disturbance for centuries

stilt-rooted trees—trees whose roots have grown above-ground on stumps, logs, or the exposed roots of toppled trees that have decayed away; this creates openings or air spaces between the roots, making them appear elevated

topography—the lay of the land, the direction slopes face and the steepness of their pitch

uphill basal scar—scar created by fire that burned a fuel pocket on the uphill side of a tree

weevil-deformed white pines—white pine trees whose terminal shoots were killed by the white pine weevil, creating trees with multiple trunks that usually start at heights between 5 and 30 feet

wind-tipped trees—young trees partially uprooted by a wind event with trunks that bow toward the sky

NOTES